If you were me and lived in...
FRANCE

A Child's Introduction to Cultures Around the World

Carole P. Roman

To my brothers Kevin, Stuart and their families:
Ma famille extraordinaire

Copyright © 2013 Carole P. Roman

ISBN: 1481032003

ISBN 13: 9781481032001

Library of Congress Control Number: 2012922016

CreateSpace Independent Publishing Platform, North Charleston, SC

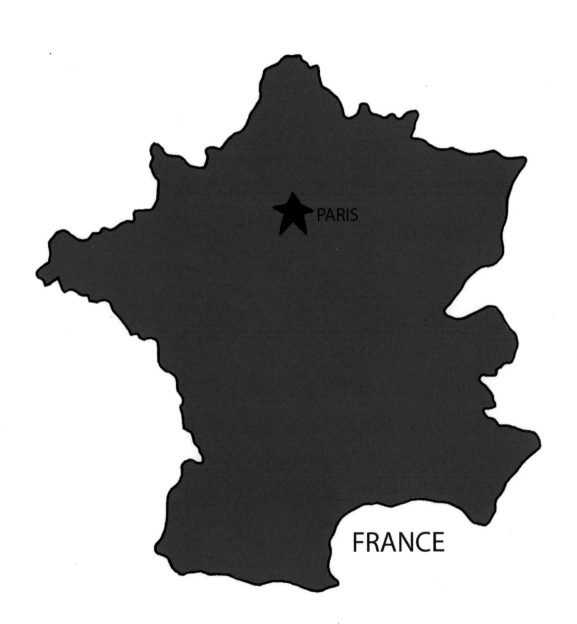

If you were me and lived in France, your home would be here in Western Europe.

2

You might live in the capital, Paris. In 1828, it was the first city in Europe to use gas lamps to light the streets, and that's how it got the nickname "La Ville-Lumiere" or the "City of Light".

Your name could be Hugo, Mathis, or Theo if you are a boy. If you are a girl, your parents might have picked Collette, Jacqueline, or Clara.

When you talk to your mommy, you would call her Maman, and when you speak to your daddy, you would say Papa.

If your parents bought bread in a boulangerie, they would pay in euros. What else do you think they would have in a boulangerie?

When friends came to visit, your first stop would be to show them the Eiffel Tower. It is an iron tower shaped like a tall, skinny triangle and built in 1889 by Gustave Eiffel. You would take the elevator to the top to see all of Paris spread out below.

Then you would go for some crepes for lunch. Crepes are delicate pancakes that can be filled with vegetables, meat, or cheese. Dessert crepes are made with fruit and dusted with sugar. Some children like their crepes with chocolate hazelnut spread, which is similar to peanut butter.

One of the most popular sports in France is soccer, but if you were me you would call it Le Football. Maybe you would just like to have a tea party with a poupée, which is a doll.

The fourteenth of July is a very special day in France. It is the French National Day, which is known to many as Bastille Day and you would celebrate it with fireworks and parades. It commemorates the beginning of the French Revolution and is very similar to America's Fourth of July.

So now you see, if you were me, how life in France could really be.

Pronunciation

Paris-(pair-EE)

La Ville–Lumiere-(la v-eil Lum-min-aire)

Hugo-(Y-OO-g-oh)

Mattieu (mat-ee-u)

Theo-(th-ee-oh)

Collette-(call-e-TTe)

Jacqueline-(JACK-uh-lynn)

Clara-(K-l-ah-r-uh)

Maman-(Ma-Man)

Papa-(pAH-p-uh)

Boulangerie-(boo-Lawn-jair-EE)

Eiffel-(Eye-Ful)

Gustave-(Goos-tav)

Poupée-(Pu-Pe)

Bastille Day-(b-AE-S-t-EE-l)

École-(e-kohl)